I0419761

A SOAK IN THE KNIGHTS

MOAT

Alexej Savreux

(No quote from Noam Chomsky this time; SORRY!!)

"Are you stoned?" "No." "You should be."

– Alexej and a metalhead at a club

Formerly titled:

<u>Workingman Poems</u>

<u>and then:</u>

<u>Scissorhands, Alexej (Asoak in the Knight's Moat)</u>

Alexej Savreux

LaTeX & like we WANT grad school, & Cigarettes Vol. I [chapbook]

"One of these days I'm going to be a grad school defector."

"Why?"

"Because . . . the way life is . . . it's all about working to death in the name of STACKING some paper, stacked, anyways. It's Love and it's Hell.

Why burn out? Unemployment and White Collar - same heads on the Seven Sister Dragon".

"Gotcha".

PeAcE.

ASOAK IN THE KNIGHT'S MOAT

© 2016 by Alexej Savreux
All Rights Reserved
First Printing: 2017
Kansas City, Kansas

Paperback ISBN:

ISBN: 9781521354070

No e-Book ISBNs applicable to this version.

Illogical Conceits

Independently Published

A LENGTHY & INFORMAL DEDICATION IN
EXTEMPORE ::

THIS BOOK IS FOR ALL THE POT SMOKING
KIDS IN COLORADO . . .
#MOTOWNFOREVA

&

LUKE & ROXY ~ AS A WEDDING GIFT ~

&

STEPHEN SANCHEZ ~ FOR BEING A BRUDDAH ~

&

SAM SPAR ~ FOR FRIENDSHIP ALL THESE YEARS ~

TABLE OF CONTENTS:

DAMN THE CONSEQUENCES; GIVE ME THE PEN!

Fuck living to be 80 -- I just want to hear the crowd ROAR!!

Anti-Kapital

"Have you read my latest book?"

"No. Not yet."

I'm not a man who thrives on EGO. But I AM a man who thrives on reward for success, *following* hard work.
That said, I am NOT a man who thrives on PUNISHMENT for failure to *complete* hard work.

"...and yet you identify as ze anti-kapitalist?"

I don't identify as nobody.

"Vhy's dat?"

"Why do you think I'm going to end up being nothing?"

"Vhy?"

"Because I could've been anything!"

A Housewife's Address Before 18th Century Congress

Shall I call attention to the plight of women who must work
and cook everyday while their husbands sit around waiting to be served?
Or should I speak about the plight of bichons and other small dogs in the house of Brian?

[applause]

The Lighthouse, a Swirling Flashlight

WiNDoWs Of The SkuLL ArE FuCKInG EmPtY.
...the Brain is also OutsiDe of the SkuLL
LiMitLeSs SwiRLInG OrB oF LIGhT, You FuCKiNG LiGhTHoUSe
ThE MaN *is* BuT a PenNinSuLa
....thE BrAin iS tHe MeTaphySiCiaN oF the SoUL

tHe SEnsEs aRe BoTh BacK & FoRtH
OrB Goosh. Gow. Wow. Woah.
Be A LigHthoUSe MaN & throw Away yOuR OaRs.

I Am . . . And From HERE.

I am from my Mutka and Brian, the Professor; I am from Isolde, a Czech ballet dancer, in Vienna, whose Father was a Holocaust survivor; I am from a long line of Slavs - the original surname: Stojanovic.
I am from Basquiat, Revere, Byron, Welsh, & Burroughs . . .
From New England - where birth certificates decide whether or not you belong.
Bucolic Northwestern Vermont, replete with beautiful foliage and autumns; lots of boats, small neighborhoods, and triple decker apartments.
I am from the land of fish and chips . . . the land of lobster, maple syrup, and Ben & Jerry's.
I am from the omerta of provincial New England pride; that small corner of the Northeast known for its fishing, working class roots, labor unions, and knockaround sports enthusiasm.
From Liberec, my beautiful Grandmother's home. From Vranja, a divided land . . . from the ballets of Vienna to the trials and pressures of pain of the Holocaust, to America as a second generation American.
I am from "New England English" - an agrammatical pidgin; Joual a Montreal and French-based creole, the wonderful word: "wicked" and long, overly drawn-out enunciations.
I am from a place where most people attend Parochial school . . . but many don't observe the Catholic tenets, and many often reject them.
I am from the non-profit world, the working man ethos, and perfectionist work ethic. I am from academia and archeology, linguistics, and anthropology.
I am from chainsmoking cigarettes, hurricanes, and the region of several "Perfect Storms" . . .
From here I sail it tight against the tide to a variety of locales, armed with an inveterate multi-tasking brain, - which sometimes may be to my own detriment. From here I am sloppy, disorganized, neurotic, and paradoxically carefree. From here I conquer schizophrenia.
From here I am laying the foundation of the rest of my life, which, of course, is probably going to change quite a bit - I am known for being eclectic.
I define Slavic pride; a language "nerd"; a man never destined to have lots of money.
I am from the harsh winters of New England and Colorado - I am not a conservative of any kind. I am a union man. And anti-capitalist.
from Wu-Tang, Lou Reed, and Nine Inch Nails
My talaria - magnetic, - a fighter who is steadfast in his determination to go every round, in every fight, quite nutty, even if he loses on all counts by points, ALONE . . . I AM ALEX.
. . . Like Conrad, Motherfucker!

////////////////

While I fundamentally disagree with your position . . .
    Huh?
Look, after I got out of the Marines I realized...EVERYONE . . HAS . . . **POWER.**

[WHAT WILL POLITICIANS SAY ONCE THEIR MICROPHONES ARE TURNED
OFF?]

    sans ----------------> **HERE.**

1 Way Phone Call to Dr. Michael Eric Dyson at Georgetown University

[This was made during a psychotic manic episode in my early twenties after I had come
up with a solution to the unified field theory, and was under the delusional hypothesis
that I had to save America . . . and the WORLD].

Brother Dyson,

This is Brother Savreux. The ToE is Vy=Xy. We can save America from the fiscal cliff.
It's called supranational non-monetary equilibrium. Call me back -- this is an encrypted
EPIRB cellphone.

Brother Savreux. OUT.

A Hypodermic in a Vein

You are neither living nor Dead
merely a jewel on mystery's crown;
your face is like a nymphy shadow;
Digging up the cold exhaust from the dying Ground
Your pearled eyes linger in realms that deify
Sight to the blind, music to the deaf,
Strength to the weak, and all Desire to Sex
Two blinking eyes flash in narcotized woe
and you exist outside a Cave of inglorious foes
On the breadth of the night's rusted wings,
Gods of parsimony unite in a cosmic matrimony
Their goddesses give birth to infantile contemperaneity
and a man dies in contentment's cradled antiquity
and life is a but a syringe full of Death
a mythical asterisk amongst the Star's ranks
its 1cc & gauge met with cantankerous skanks!
& its spoon to be the fissional division
Like an atom parceled in a box of toys
& its half-hearted security an honest conviction

of your poppied needle screaming in your fat vein
nothing but a screeching willow
an opiate who seldom dreams of cannabis
and a dazed head on Destiny's Pillow,
milky dew found, head hit the ground
Let the lights dance, headrush in a trance
Nothing's changed, but your gaze is eviscerated
A Galactic birth of a Godly changeling
Wrought Seas of black soot, bringing time
to my stately home in the scented Sun
where the end eventually brings everyone
and I am sure of nothing but methadone's desire
Beyond oblivions whimpering apocalypse
Like a caryatid unworthy of her pillar
Lies in an immutable pale Horse that can't be tamed
and an ecstasy stolen by villains
Just like a fat needle screaming in a fat vein!

The Sad Jewel Box

slight box now thick and self-contained
...emerges like an infant clasping,
lashed to the confines of noble ambitions,
would if it could be enough to collect
in the intrepid silence of the womb,
that thou wouldst wish a heart dry of treasure
so by the moon's melodious light may flash again,
& thou be deaf & mute see *here*: *a morose of gold*

ALL GOOD ART SHOULD MAKE YOU SUICIDAL.

Jack the Ripper

Why does the baker bake the bread?
        Why did Jack the Ripper cut off heads?
Fucking obvious: everyone needs a snack.

WILL THERE BE ENOUGH WATER FOR ALL OF US TO DROWN?

....

"I'm really good at not complimenting myself."

-- a potential girlfriend; in conversation (I didn't call her again)

....

The Sub-Minimum Wage Slave Class

Why encourage disaster . . . ruled by dollar, Almighty.
       Enjoy every sandwich, it's all we got.
Praises bided to Warren Zevon, that wiseman knew a lot.
 Lunch break and smoke break, slowly kills us.
But still we work.
Some of us; homeless...

Proverbial Variation II.

I. Gandhi was full of shit, or somethin'
   A. Like he didn't know how to articulate his vision!

'Be the change you wish to see in the world?'

       Huh? I think that was it.
How about: 'initiate the change that needs to be effected?'
Duh.

Bourgeois

What dorito-eating youth conferred with dopest luxuria
Courts a-many on the vernal petals of a well cured plant, full
   Bit, the lips of habits, acquiring timeless buds instant of thou
   In garlands thy silky black hair, adored and elaborated odours, aloft
Paid in thy sorted pipes uplifted? O now oft he smokes
On play his several savant gods complain: and on his knees
   Rough with his back's blood, red liquid scathed
   Undaunted shall desire,
 enwomb ye cockles, of things both terrific and odd,
Whose mind like a lotus always vacant always utterly diluted with a lucid aim
   Hopes ye; of erotic tales, and profitable sales
   Mindful; Helpless they
To whom thou seem'st care, hung by coarse lungs in vows exclaimed
Point the cigarette's grey smoke then declares't time has been hanged
   Their ephemeral needs, like a garden plucked free of pot smoking thieves
   Unforseeable, discernable only to the amiable God of Weed.

The Success of a Failed Direction

Yo, destiny is as soft as time on course,
        My point is flawless, truth invades from afar
Whether strength invades, an animal, disgusted.
Our rears cooking up in me...befriending unknowledge.
        The fatal Eagle flies like a minimum wage booty
 Always chasing tail, on the make.
And we die like a germ in a dope selection of anti-bacterial handwash.
Corporate Americas, inclined.

Tombstone ~ Wisdom

May my pieces be with you.

        TIME DESTROYS US ALL
Evolution...Adapt. Evolve.

But I'm not going to die without having some scars to show St. Peter that I tried living.

Et tu Soleil?

...Even the New Son, rises like the Literatures of all the Majestic Scriptures
        & the Girls, like all the Women of Mercy

Dopest Professors & their Broke, Obedient Proteges

Workers unite, the SOC dudes
given the chance to accrue Wisdom
        The Sun of Men & Women full of many salivas,
 a symphony of blissful hell - Masters of being subordinates,
                Equivocal, Residual - Despised underlings.
A constitution is but a tear . . .
and a shift to a working man is a hundred years.
        The education is never was or is . . . the reprimand,
the wake-up in the form of loud music,
endless cycles of night & work & course
        strapped down, lawless, pathologically lawful
you, O Brother, -- fucking whipped.

UnSent Elegy to Heath Ledger, who Nailed Hebephrenia

Heath, thespian extraordinaire,

...as a 2X year old who has experienced Hebephrenia, I tip my psycho looking B-Ball Hat to ye.

you nailed it. I do not agree with the agent of chaos mentality, but your psyche your senseless laughter, your fascination with CHAOS, stripping away the egos of authority, your heartfelt & honest portrayal of those afflicted with insanity, WOW. what a thing you gave us, what a Legacy you left, and I am NOT being insincere,

Easily the greatest Batman villain EVER. You rocked it, man. You fucking nailed it.

The Dark Knight is an Exceptional Movie. One of the greatest Performances, Cinema will ever know . . . and Cinema has absolutely **nothing** to **threaten you with!**

I liked your wardrobe, I oughta know, they paid for mine as well, & now I know why

I'm always **SMiLiNG** . . . . Because a **Joke** is Funny!

Smile your **Glasgow SMiLE**

WHY   SO   **SERIOUS?!**

Unrequited Letter to Dr. John Forbes Nash Jr.

It should be stated that I have a mild syndrome that resembles some form(s) of schizophrenia, bipolar disorder, and A.D.D. And I also have synesthesia. My psychiatrist thought for awhile that I may actually have had just the world's most bizarre case of catatonic schizophrenia, although this was later hesitantly ruled out (I, personally, don't discount it at all). Here's a letter to Dr. John Forbes Nash Jr. about my equation (for the unified field theory) from 2013, when I was 24 years old (I'm now 27 years old):

ToE

$Vy=Xy$

Dr. Nash,

My name is Alex Savreux, i have Childhood Onset Disorganized Schizophrenia, Bipolar Psychosis, & Oineroid Syndrome. The ToE is $Vy=Xy$. My nickname is Alexej. I wish very much to correspond (& more hopefully) meet you soon. We have much in common, & i, unequivocally believe it would be 'time travel'.

With Immeasurable Admiration of your Work, Story & Courage,

your friend,
Alex

:)

////////////////////////////////////

No response. *tear* I'm probably far cuckooier than he ever was. He was ill. I'm just BATSHIT.

tear x2

facepalm

...or, as Armen said: **"...you're playing the game of life in hard mode".**

I didn't know what he meant but he explained to me that it was video game terminology.
And that "hard-mode" was a mode for gamers designed to keep the game going and keep it "interesting"
...so that they don't get "bored".

Aughh...

Title

I want my body lying in a field so that I can be eaten.
Let the birds eat me.
I want my Death to come full circle with nature.
I want to give life as I absorb Death. Yes, merci.
R.I.P. to the posses of this world
(and to Jim Morrison). :P

Slice Meat

[to the tune of Black Flag's "Black Coffee"]

Bar Chords/Bar Codes ----> here [get it?]:

SONG:

> Slicing meat in a deli
> Slicing meat in a deli
> Slicing meat in a deli
> Slicing meat in a deli

Stare at the clock

> Slicing meat in a deli
> Slicing meat in a deli
> Slicing meat in a deli
> Slicing meat in a deli

Stare at the clock
Stare at the clock
Through my hand goes the slicer
Sliced through my HAND MY HAND my HAND
Slicer!

About that thing called Suicide:

Mortality is inevitable; CONTROL is NOT!!

Frozen Sun

Sometimes I wonder how many Suns there have Been, soft, mellow tobacco balls of fire illuming the world bright with sunshine & light, & beautiful twilights, flashing their passionate gaze upon the unsuspecting world. I lay sometimes, in a hammock just to let the Sunlight sink in, I love sunlight & it provides me with a warm heart, but the Sun is frozen in time, unable to dissociate or escape, sort of like a tasteless tongue, stuck in the mouth of animal with fangs; everything equals perfect. But if that Sun doesn't last long neither will the multitudes of others surrounding it & sometimes I wish to lay down on silk or satin, jasper -- velvet even, & absorb its amorously drifting waves of permanance worthy of Latin . . . yeah.

SPHERE FOR BLUE COFFEE

There ain't no wrong key!!
    Smoke that reefer, blow that smoke, take that benzedrine.
Why? 'Cuz there ain't no wrong key!
Oh, my! Cats beware, you're in for some fun in this hallowed town o' mine...
I done seen bee–bop on down the square and on Vine.
And there ain't no wrong key.
    I've travelled this great land of ours.
Searched this wild soul o' mine.
And babe, there simply ain't no wrong key...
       I been stuck in psych wards,
I been played Hell down the line
I been hardcore, I been on a ledge, struggled with this role of mine.
    Seen the red rivers and unrelenting engines of time.
And I've heard the ghettos and slums & desperations of the mind.
    But baby, don't worry, we ain't on trial, ya know why?
Because you be who you be, in this grand World of rhymes!

Chaps and chicks, be forever slick,
    and free, 'cos in life...there ain't no wrong key.

In life there ain't no wrong key; it's about how you put the notes together, B.

Ain't no wrong key.
Ain't no wrong key.
Ain't no wrong key.
Ain't no wrong key.

Q.E.D.

THIS IS THE END: FOR YOU -- DRUNKEN, OLD FRIEND; THE END.

If I Had an Irregular Head & Were a High Renaissance Master

I have an irregular head, muse & vassal & as I slept on naked silk,
 with my mistress by my side,
 I transposed I separated from my body & combusted out of existence,
temporarily, in my new self of non-existence,

I decided to paint all night & into the day, so I went forth,
 & I left rhyming schemes to the Poor, I picked up my paintbrush
and I invested (decided to paint) brownish icicles on my commanding canvas
 & I gave (painted) the angelic Girls Orange-plaid Wings,
& little Girlish smiles, & their frizzy Hair Augmented their affections Still!
& their Special Grins, livened the raw hands of my self-created jowl! ~
But as I sifted unhearted grins on their innocent, glowing Smiles,
I thought of the painless edict of God's own Eden,
The Freedom Nest's own hyped-up fortress mote on the grand dawn hearth & the
didactic grey clouds beyond all the Suns that Float!

Computer Hackers, Artful

The new cowboys! The vigilantes! The beauty, O Beauty!
	Such night spread like a hemisphere,
So beautiful your binaries and deception, floating, ominous music
	& threats, a-Trojan ~ disembodied voices. . .
B.A. such education, immaculate. Courage. Tattoos. Cigarettes, yank goes the hacker!
   D-DoS B.S. ~ Boom! A website fucked up. A tide turned, like a mathematical prodigy
snorting lines of linear and co-linear algebra. D-DoS...you ARE immense, O villains of
the
	noblest Heart, - routine, immaterial...and maniacal laughter, aloft
Shoot me in the foot and corral the rest.
   The union shall one day thank you.

TheRe is an eSsence; [although]

I remember it well broseph.
  When, as a brother - my hand became hard and viable
Ain't nothing like breaking even to even the ugly music of ourselves
 the unions a blunder, lastly, evenings baffled under the weight of discipline,
patience, and broken humility style star lilies.

Like a good bassist - We knew when to play:
..and we knew when not to play....
  We lived for everything, and yet lived for nothing.
We believed in nothing and yet believed in a few things;
  We, against lots of A LOT, - but not believing in any one, true, thing.
	Except the rules ablaze with the disunion of the many cries for another forever
 our heads stacked in empirical reality & our many songs,
still singing a song unsung, wishful for the radiant benefit of a social floor
	and less humility. Breaking even was no big thang.

  . . . we were still ROCKSTARS.

And that's been the ESSENCE of our America.

So, this is "Life"

So, this is LIFE.
Nothing this year. EVERYTHING NEXT YEAR.
      THEN, NOTHING THE FOLLOWING YEAR.
Christmas sometimes SUCKS. fohr da workinhgmahn.

Let's smoke hookah & pretend we weren't living paycheck to paycheck
            Bubbly, Bubbles . . . So, we have mo' money
And Manager giveth, manager taketh away.
High-end - manufacturing a pseudoexistence for those dispossessed.

      Christmas is always better . . . NEXT YEAR.

Does Santa Claus forget the kids?

Aughh . . .

V. StressnesS lvl.

...and yet Capitalism NEVER STOPS! NEVER!
      No wonder people are dropping dead of heart attacks non-stop
It's axiomatic; a RUSH & nothing EVER, EVER STOPS!

Time Destroys Us All.

RAISE THE FLAG

I want to be the Black Flag of Poetry!
      Get in the van!!
Hardcore, initial. Instead, inside decide the incite
  Now you're back & I'm a FLAG . . .
Not the Raphael, Basquiat, or Banksy of language
 . . but the motherfuckers who can barely play but don't care COS THEY ROCK IT!
      I'll replace the mothafuckin' flag!
Poor grammar and overwhelming syntax, yea
  Long live me ye pirate punk! Poeta; Fuckin' raise that FLAG!!

"The Sea Sage"

An Unmetered Epyllion

(LARGELY UNFINISHED)

By

Alexej Savreux

In 19th Century Massachusetts, a gravely ill Isaac Taylor lies on his deathbed vainly trying to recount to his wife Michaela and his Brother, Hezekiah Taylor, the extraordinary adventures he had in the Asiatic Regions of the World after his Whaling Ship, the 'Jack O'Lantern', ran aground near Japan. Told from the perspective of Hezekiah, who finds in Isaac's closet, a mysterious Jar with a Note, that simply reads 'For Hereafter the Jack O'Lantern Burns'. Hezekiah begins a-brooding as to what his Brother witnessed and why it has left him near Death.

Hezekiah
Isaac
Michaela
Ayida
Tatsuya
Zepheniah
Ayida
Luke
Joshua
Savannah

Book I O My Vanity!
Book II Stocking Hat Spirits
Book III Homeless in Nantucket   (Unfinished - Not included)
Book IV Christmas on the Cape   (Unfinished)
Book V Ayida, my Ayida!   (Unfinished)
Book VI Visions of the Pacific   (Unfinished)
Book VII The Voyages   (Unfinished)
Book VIII Shinto Episodics   (Unfinished)
Book VX As the Sun Weeps   (Sort of Unfinished - Not included)
Book X Twilight   (Sort of Unfinished - Not included)

Book I.

O, My Vanity!

I.

O Shone in the ray of sunlight it did a-come thru this holy stain glass tile
Resting on blanket quills piously drifting, and speaking in euripus lips
Of the covered, dank bed in yellow hue whilst thy dreams dance in ethereal skies
Speaking of violent treasons of petrific oceans and hearths of the Sun
Those New England Stars and muses who nourish like milky dew thru his veins
Stirring the appeal of a trammeled mass and its lewd flowery fusions
From the iron isle's union springs the human race and its beguiled Son
the breasted lovers of monsters flying on the wings of wild illusions,
My! How the Sun thrusts sprinkling immortal light on the Sea's great cusp
Below that glistering edifice lays the colossal abyss of the Sea
I hear Salacia singing sleepless Carols o'er the Marble Carpet of its Swells
Rising and falling with their dreams and hearts full of fresh treasures
I invoke ye, show ye great principled visions of a grand new beginning
Recount to me my memories from whatever source you choose for I am unsure
Lest this world crumble and my heart lays to waste in death's fetid breath
Where on the coast of all things royal and tremendous my brother did
Speak of softened flesh and sunny eyed optimistic destiny, there there!
Ease thy will, I say! Become your Freedoms! And how could I not foresake this endless
Ride while every morning without paradise is torture, these steeped books,
Of heart wrenching departures on whale ships remind me of those
Fabulous, prescient summer nights, nights of words, fearless nights of letters
We'd walk on those boardwalks and abscond with maturing poppies
Aye, I shall submit my own bits of knowledge which I shall impart on ye
By recounting, O muse, of the most distressing and extraordinary voyage
A travail into the impassive heart of the mysterious steel clad Buddhists
O I fear I have lost all that I had held dear for so very long and now I am distant
What task, proferred, unbarred in haste? From what stream dost success flow?
Am I to realize too late that an incendiary flame of endurance fails to ignite?
There is no sense in worrying about the present because the past controls all
Lying face down on thy bed, Michaela pulls down the shades roughly
And speaks not a word about the ill and ailing Isaac who smokes his pipe
Recollecting of his limbs that were themselves made to die into infinity
This woman cannot see the plight of his kind, nor the majesty of Heaven's Light
Shut up in the custody of a tomb, a prison of darkening and tightening might
As the mystery of life is entangled in all his raucous pursuits
He is fain for freedom even when the immortal light of liberty is extinguish'd
But I sit here before thy helpless brother and see as his constitution fails him

Yet I worry that hadn't I been there perhaps he could have been saved

II.

O how my illusory feathers take flight o'er a decedent's ecumenical deaths
Ah, as the Great Lover drizzles a backless tear flown as the rains like cobwebs
Down thy icy, inscrutable drain, trace dry of any mirthful, betroth'd company
None of Ours, most disdainful exploitations could hinder any of thy Fates
As always, Great Lover, paces to and fro, the window and exclaims tenaciously
O, but say ye Isaac, O but say ye, what and how sick you are, such Discord!
Immensely your travels, hast promised great fortune upon ye, ineptitudes bare
Fallen beneath thy breast of inferior workings, like a pillowless Bed, with no Gate
Unmade, and wrongly disheveled, many a-time thru came this windowless Light
And ye b'een sent to eat thy meals as I laboriously prepare thy meal to feed ye,
Nobody on this here Home of Ours, hast ever complained of incompetencies
O Great Lover, ceases the details of Isaac and he lay there in his contentment
Desirous he knew of nothing but open waters, and then, being horridly sick
He choked out a few broken words that gave to all his poor dire disposition
A new, joyous illustration his crackling, coughing chords swollen in languages
And he possessed little to no intensity or vitality, yet he was there, too undamaged
And he sought to release his deluged breath, near on a trance, and he fought
Hard for his Brethren who hath already been bewildered by their Gracious Master,
Their maker their ineradicable Holy makers and their compact Messiahs
O, Michaela, Great Lover, I have tried to reap the Virgin Truths of Asiatic Paradise!
I have so aptly sown the relished cane I stole from my Fathers, reaping Ruin!
And my Fathers before my Father's Father, like ye we planted their earned cane
deep in the woody grounds of the colored paisley pastures of Massachusetts!
O, Lord! O, Lord! Undone, Unbroken remains my colorful musings and bidings
Thy vanity! O, Brother I shall let the sojourn speak for itself, this fretful island!
Because I think it able yet be it not its colonial mouth spoken in vibratory tongues
O ye unborn rebellious, the quagmire is a specific dilemma of a difficult variety,
I am unsure of locales excepting my sextant on the Earth and because of incapacity,
We were made to exist within the confines of this here, this . . . ye old isle,
Which hast thou too been of great comfort and solace to both friend and family,
But I am indeed a Soul of vision and temperament, I did not elevate myself to the Lord
I simply went to God, and I found He, I couldn't be a bit more indelicate, Love.
I am weary, I am tired, my travels have made me tired, vixen you are to my health,
O, my Love, I could sleep for centuries, I do not wish to regret but I shan't make ye
your wheat and grace thy nestling's sky to find ye more garb and delicious delectations
I can't stand thy breathing, so heavy, lest I feign to produce some gorgeous miracle,
By the will of thy Creator, I doubt I'll see any more sprinkled sunlight ag'en, askance
Letting low and lying, as I lay in this pitiful state, lest my will break free, I must!
O, I must! O I must! I must! I must! I must! Can I not then, eat in Peace & Companies?
the Great Lover, as a beautiful fleshed Angel, swarthiest of all desires, and graces
downward places upon the fanciful divan, the nymph murmors before him
but the journeyman with a shrill moan sighs next to her, intent on a century of Sleep.

O the vanity, of humane indiscretions, such woe to ye, Brother of Mine, ye unconquered
Isaac, my Brother, ye shan't e'er be displaced by disloyalties of misfortunate lotteries
Rest by corner on Cot, let sink to a Century's Sleep, thus dictated by wife of Seafarer.

Book II.

Stocking Hat Spirits

I.

So casual, and so necessary became the trappings of self-exploration and dependents
'twould be enough of a million Ghosts, fraught with the Cape's foremost Splendor,
She slowly sang, and sang lowly Songs, the beach combed like the Hair of Aphrodite
Those disunions of severant Pirates and Savants, many thousand centurians prior
Came back to haunt and mistake ye for a Savant Ghost of child like Lunacy and Love,
Wool Caps and ungodly amounts of Tobacco swollen in the Bird Nests of Clay Pipes
Sitting still like the Sand near the Vineyard wallowing in the sorry Life sans Destiny
Lo, yet ye all seem to be but a Ghost, shroud clouded by mystic effluence and memory
Entertaining horrid amusements and syndromes of perpetual thoughts and daydreams
Atop the great Iceberg of monumental Cliffs, shown here the Mount as laid out, Biblical
So for, us to see so far, and yet wonder not about the destruction of unwanted divorces
Loving and Hating simultaneous, waxing the wanes upon Dames,
O, for ye own Damozel, my Muse on High here this ye Mount, allow one destroyed,
And Sink the wreckage of the useless ship and raise that great, bountiful anchor
As I dream and know by the seashore in years of yore and gracious hymns of yesteryear
Best are the moments yet to become, yet to be and transpire, yet to remember and
succeed
What to disregard and what to discount categorically you nefarious sentimentalist
Brethren,
O pitiable sentient descendant of all philosophical tapestries combined by flinching
laughter
Made whole undeleted by the marked frames of consistent soft plyings of spiritual
carpentry
Unless I make real, my own ambition and shackle like unchained restraints into Rapture
Does aye, Brother of ailing Brethren comb the Sands lifting and lurching forward for all
Laughter?
Shall I walk until I find the nestling sky lost in the colossal abyss of mystical schisms?
Asiatic Paradise, O Steel Clad Buddhists and Softest Clay and Marble Swells, O, lo, lo, lo,
From when do I return and when do I refuse and what shall I say when ag'en in front of
Muse?
That I, but lonesome Brother of Brethren stunned by illness and the all encompassing,
Refute the wishes that preceded thine own coming of age, thine own ponderings and
tedious questions?
I think it not so, yet ye know well enough of the good and the bad to be forever pining
both

To be ever for and heretofore as ill as all and as wanting and ambitious as a builder of Ships

O, Steel Clad Buddhists and window panes of Church Lights, ye know my nobility, So, Dazing the mysteries of diffident aptitudes and loathesome ambitions my laughter, not So!

I wave to the many Goblins and Ghosts of the Servants of these breathtaking Shores

Pity it be, that I am never returned with a simple nod or a gesture of thou being inconsolable

Alas, so wicked and unknowable scrooges of the Captain's Crew, done without the doing

Perspiring without the Sweat and chewing on the hackery of the calculated martials of prophecy

II.

I am here now, riding the pounding Horse through the forlorn pastures of our Settlement

And yet, so below me pronounces the Pull of undesirable modern acquirements of my Eye

Sallow, my shagged Spirit, Bless'd with the Stocking Hat and the Rain absent of the Sail

Broken Settlements in our new towns and O, thru his inward projecticles were his Seeings

Standing in the closet of staring sights and blaringly loud, obnoxious nights with no armor

I am all alone on this Beach and yet I feel the tug of all Stocking Hat Spirits Past, memorized

Ergo and mace hereso by the enunciation of dubious intrigue and the piercing of Isaac's legend

I am going to bury his Body by the Beach if he does infected doth die, and he to be eaten by pidgeons

An appropriate Death for a Man of just being on the float'n leaky raft of excoriating duty

Following throughout the deathless pastures of our seeing Pastures, so Free follows our Seeing

O, Muse, to be but a castaway on an island, to be a native in your own Prison, a casket of stupors

Quaker I am your fizzl'd dreaming workings sidewalked beach as peach'd dusk atop white night

and black morning overwhelms the misadventures and misunderstandings of every Brotherhood.

I am the only Legacy of sonless Brother and daughterless his Wife and yet declared is the aloof

So be it, O marshalled, conniving Muse, I do not take seriously the disciplinerian of the misled.

The Afternoon here, is neither Black nor White, but a celestial rainbow of grains of both Sand & Soot.

Wit & Witticism

Art is the OPPOSITE of "academic"
      -- you fucking dumbass!!

Daniel; Daniel; Daniel B.

A whistle of street music enlivens the blacktopped streets, portraying it as slightly sunburnt, as the streets were red as naked flesh keeping out the twisted and winding drafts, paralyzing the proletariat, and shuttering the freezing, whose limp and nimble bodies, sifted frost, from the playful clouds from above, winding and whistling, a great tune, fed up with the vision as it rises high up above the knees of the storyteller, his mouth opened, and then closed with enormous fission, diffusing the light of a sacred star, that fiendish immediacy where delusion spoke of fractured beauty, an essence of thought, a disaster of immediacy and a denizen of languid, deteriorating intellect.

Pretentious & Unpretentious, Mothafucka!!

Oh, Hi effete pretense, you don't watch movies, only "films"?

      Well, I don't read newspapers -- I only read *books*.

[Alex's Brain]:: Hmmmm....how can we fuck up Alex's day today?

                  How about we make him think pastrami is going to eat him alive?
That works.

            We'll go with THAT.

/////////

I know a dude. He's a Ph.D. candidate in astrophysics. He just likes to BLAZE and just talk NON-STOP about astrophysics.

He's like:

Wha????

[EXhALe . . .]

Ballers & Slackers

There are several different kinds of employees. The kind that kick ass and are fucking sexy with their work; the kind that mean well but underperform . . the kind that slack, and make excuses; and the downright BALLERS.
Tha dude's who rock DEIR SHIT.

The Violin of Mozart

O nimble hands on such surface,
do not caress the gem of flight
music you wish to hear tonight
may not wish you to ever hear
it may refuse you stupors drink
or flaunt tempestuous success
austrian architecture ensconce
the mortal shaft of curved strings
the strings of aenonian music
that forever succeeds remains
shall play in your evenings prayers
and if you fill the gauntlet of human want and urge
may you know to play the notes that are forever agleam
in the genius of knowledge

Catalepsy & Fantasy Part I, II, & Redux

1.

I think as though I am in a strait jacket
an immodest luxury to cometh, an emotionless sigh
cigarettes on the dazed, occult sofa
Glass pipes, the momentum of history is heathen,
Because she doesn't die
Sublime, she may be, perfect figurine, (at last I have seen!)
& Brazenly, I remove my logical monocle

2.

A glass eye she screams & ends the darkest of nights
Maggots await, unbroken knot, time is stuck
& vanity is quite illuming & ill
Zounds adhere! Be still! Charity's prosperity!
A mouthful of sex strapped in luck
Right before a blighted dawn, my vigil alerts a street light & iron rain
I cometh to right before the incurious wrong

3.

Neither heaven nor hell shall ably tell
My mystery ends in a swell, a riot of periled calculus
Its own psyche is ignorant, self-effacing
Like a biography transient, a vision's utterance
Suns! A loud fluttering, drone by the seaside
A disaster upon the disheveled ears of yore!
Spells that shall impart wisdom upon folklore

4.

& the knees that clash, oft past suicide's grasp
Joker hats on those jackals!
A great length of rope shall hang them from their doom's mast!
The elements of idleness slowly arose
& those idiots have swindled my love, & eaten her bones
I am still, unheard & unrecognized by tongue
Sleight of hand shall entrance, anti-implants

5.

Past all opiated Afghani perfumes & Tibetan oils
I have become a self-seeking, sustainable pariah!
To vanish from the land, like a handful of sand
A mast with no evident sail; winds, noise stuttering soft & low
& Chemistry is so obviously prevalent, a calamity of design
How it embraces, dislocates, & retraces a damozel

6.

She is history's magnifico song, canto, an opera!
A chain smoking almah & style cunning, a fiend!
I am a conjurer of the stoned & communal audience
A fantastic spectacle, in an unending hour glass
I awoke to the tribunal, a haze, I light a candle
& Right before my eyes she sullenly awakes
Upon her shivering breast plate, I eat the first bleat

7.

Much she affords me, though I could never offend her
But brought on by time's nuisance, a relative construct
I'd laugh until my rioting rubbed itself out
But she doesn't dream in miscellaneous ways
She is the vain, incalculable, modern desirous
She is a modern lover, born of incredible, nubile hands
Don't forget her past loves became the damned

8.

But could such a tortured eye bare to sulk?
In infamous interrogations, knotted like discarded silk
& Once in a great while, my droning eye could transcribe
Down in history, with a vile pen & a vial of iniquitic juice
Just so much to destroy a submissive self, like art
I never had the balls to cum oil masterpieces
Galvanizing, she left in a brothel of despair

9.

'tis whereupon she discovered some crystalline dares
Unfair, she climbs up the side, like a virus that rides
on top of ye, unafraid of hell soaked, improper, pisces
She, above all else is made of those which a-soak
Don't forget the harmonica breath as it wept & I awoke
So calm thy veils for once in awhile
She breathes & bleeds with song, til I crack a smile

10.

Crafting an affair, in arrears like a commodity with a fetish
She is also solo gone, the days of rear worn comedy down
She is illogical, I am saintly, infirm & charm'd
But whence does this propensity eek to flow?
Unconscious she does it again, & I beg for a moan
Quite witless I am, but then again what is it to you, friend?
I hold a revolver to my head, I am electrified, inculcated

11.

& with this 36 caliber machine & unself creator
I spin the galactic chamber, inside a bullet like a universe

Makes for the best of loving, on trial, like a felon
I click out for the time being, nobody though will ever get out
She checks the bullets, I pull on the strong winds
I nail myself to the wall like a hypodermic parasite
I'm told to run, but I haven't got the legs

12.

I'm no longer worthy of her downtrodden gait
If pleasure be the meeker, & the seer the cleaner
Then perhaps we should strive to behold a believer
Right in the cockles of our palms
Til she bleeds & bleeds & there's grass growi'g on the lawn
This be your domain, your infantile crown & just
You have swayed young fiend, to the infinity of dust!

13.

I have cut off both of my hands so I cannot masturbate
It's how I will come alive in the future
My belief in self-torture is only a fractured, dissident eye
Witnessing the trickery, horrors, & vestals of time
A eunuch should be allowed to attain that mystical gain
Whereupon love is aptly misplaced
& then! Ah, yes, for that definitive emotion! I shall no longer guess thy cursed name!

14.

I am a nobler man than I was in those days
Just the same, I was torn apart leaving maggots in my brain
they gnawed & gnawed, my brain outgrew their game
like a chessmaster destroying a checker playing gnome,
as neurotic as a court jester smoking the rock of crack
and yet there I amazed, awaiting an injection of something to bring me back
. . . and I lay in that trance, in that dream, in that amazement,
for a momentary eternity . . . never having once realized the difference.

RaFaeLi

A Prose Poem of Infectious Beauty & Cataclysmic Science

PaRt 1. The Manifesto of the Professional

Shall I begin thus?

I confess that I possess a legacy that is crazily aberrant. I could be described as being a self-styled master of cultural erudition, a neurotic, uneasy, pill popping designer drug maker, with a penchant for making off the cuff spiels, as well as some brazenly idiosyncratic observations. I am obsessed with chemistry, specifically pharmaceuticals, and I drink chloral hydrate as if it were the elixir of the Gods. I also confess that I have been a coarse, vulgar, & unsophisticated connoisseur of cataclysmic beauty. I saw all sexual items as a mystical caveat, worthy perhaps only of Zeus or the immortal light of those few parsimonious brain cells devoted to compartmentalizing dopamine and pleasure. I am a relentless infidel in my endless pursuit of objectifying all that is beautiful. I like art, but I never had the creative balls to cum masterpieces. I left that for the abject and disenfranchised intellectual fuckups who had nothing better to do with their time then toy with oil and film. I have always loved music, but it is irregular music that interests me. I like noisy, unorthodox jazz, with lots of crazy, atonal feedback and arrhythmic time signatures.

I am guilty of adhering to these whimsical faculties during sexual dalliances and conquests and exploits of a unanimously untoward nature, driving the inane, puritanical stereotypy of society insane, until my physician (a boorishly self-analytical girlfriend) criticized my odd sex technique and dubbed my playful, classless antics with a diagnosis of putrid, venereal disease, a virus of the mind. In all my life I had purposefully engendered a lifestyle that disavowed the inability to transcend time and space. I found that physics was the only relevant pursuit to a life devoted solely and without falter to truth, and I believed truth and beauty to be inextricably and irresistibly bound by the same omnipotent roots, both highly organic and indissoluble and altogether making cohesive study more profitable. But it was not greed that drove my scientific or unsavory libido, no not in the least, for I was foremost a philanthropist, a disaffected secularist on a humanitarian mission with a primordial vision to accomplish the impossible. To look the impossible odds of impending doom squarely in the eye and meet with slight self-empowerment an equation that would prove the impossible--beauty is forever a thoughtful, classy, and noble aspiration. Henceforth I shall refer to beauty and immortality as being all but dissimilar.

Crack is FUCKING cheaper . . . perhaps I should call RaFaeli to Dinner? We will smoke . . . & talk of things, yes, & then that discotechque will sound like surround sound. It will be like the ennui of pleasure.

. . . but no ennui for swooning; & no pleasure for ennui.

///////////////!////////////

Fuck differential ekalz. I JUST WANT TO WORK WITH COMPUTERS!!

He Had a Crazy Eye!

I died once. I awoke from my Death on a highway of cold, smokey caves; with Jesus saying: "You don't belong here." Suddenly, I got into a cab, the driver had a crazy, lazy eye and he asked: "Where to?" He drove me to Hell. Suddenly, I awoke. But then, as I was waking…I saw my psychiatrist looking down at me after ECTs while I was still lying on my bed:

      and, and, an, ..he..he..he HAD A CRAZY EYE!!!

Ahhhhh!!

[Terrified schizophrenic patient runs out of the room and just before hitting a wall, falls forward into a slouching catatonic stupor]

/////////////////////////////////

This is the solution to the unified field theory of physics: $Vy=Xy$

/////////////////////////////////

Hours for a Handful of Dimes

Nor, too, does humanism count for much amid
these stressfucks.
  Going to work is like going to WAR.
The line is always: "What can I use ya fohr?"
  Tha more you get it out, the more you got to get in MORE.
You trade away your life for money, to try and live
  and that's about all ya get; sometimes, life feels like SHIT.
But we're working anyway, cos it's a RUSH & a REWARD.
Fuck that communism shit. It's boring and doesn't work.
  Just gotta make time and a half FIRST.
Also, what about breaking even? Welcome to our Worlds.
  We'll get there. In the mean time, don't let your truck break down
Fill your tanks..grab some Taco Bell & a Dew, smoke a cig…
Love Life. There's a Buddhist essence here, askance, - the workingman is the
enlightened man.

Fiene!!

DIAGRAMS

DIAGRAM 1A

```
19 Oct. 2012              /CIRCUMVENT
                         /
                        /


CONGRESS ------------->              <------------ CONGRESS

                        PERVERSION
                           ^
                        INVERSION

   <-------------REGRESS [VERSION] PROGRESS ------------>

                        CONVERSION
                        REVERSION
                           ^
                        SUBVERSION
CONGRESS ------->  ^              <---------- CONGRESS

                              /
                             /
                            /


                     CICURMNAVIGATE


Abstraction - Theorem - Purport - Purport Concrete - Theory - Proof ->

[ ABSOLUTE ]
```

DIAGRAM 1B

```
                              Temple --> Top
  ^
axiomatica
www.illconceits.org
Aphrodite Goddess ---> - woman
Pro ---> abundance
Anti ----> [absence]
A <---> (non) <---> absence
Non <---> absence
OOOOOOOOO CIRCLES
tabular                                  MIRRORS Obama ----->
V
Globe - Bumper Sticker - By the People - For the People - Of the
People X
"Materialist Topicalities on the Paradox of Identity"
Chart (in extempore) infinite mnemonic devices ad infinitum -
every discipline/field
(perpetrate) Eastern Orthodox Christianity
(affix)
i
-(profix)- Ecumenical Proof!
/
defix
sub
fix grater /               ( WORLD WIDE WEB )
ate
hate                       [WWW.--> MULTI VERSE PROOF DUH! ]
dis
plate
- BASE THEORY THE -        ----    ^
- MISAPPROPRIATIONS OF EQUAL SIGNIFICANCE
- ------> SELF-NEUTRALIZING ----> [VERSION] ------->
```

DIAGRAM 1C

22. Oct. 2012 1:58 PM GEB SP E JCCC, KS

```
^
}                   "infinity & beyond"
iconoclast
/~                  <-- AXIOMATICA -->          { BVERBMENT
                                                  BVEVERBALITY
                                                  VEREARRANGEEARR
                                                  VVABRRBREAN
                                                  VERBBRERBAGEGY
                                                  RBAAEVANME
                                                  LNGEANT }
Conductor
Orchestrator
/
(string)
symphony             easy- see thru - TRANSPARENT
sound
harmony
/
/     SOUND                 (invert &) - Musical symbols


(Archetype
Stereotype                       [Infinite Dimensions]
Prototype)

<----------------------------------->

Generic           )
/                        )
/                            )
BELOW                          )
homogenous           ORBIT /////////// } Radio --------->

/    Frequency              (Wavelengths) ) ) ) )

below                          )
                             )
/                    [ CARTOGRAPHICAL OBLIVION ]
                             )
dif. manifestations & representations
"immortality" ) )
cyclical everything
ALL I GOT IS TIME! (LITERALLY)
```

Unfinished Christmas Letter to Stephen "Brothabear" Sanchez

Sage Stephen,

     Ah, the enthusiastic bells of charity ring loud! Ah, yes! 'Tis the season to be in love with all the wonderful, prodigious, & beautiful affections that are bound tight within us, let them out, give into all sincerity, all charity, all prosperity, embrace the yearly change! For we are the prophets of an indefinable & (to our detriment) elusive gate keeper who holds all those secrets & mystery intact. We must harbor, within ourselves, a fundamental desire to improve the quality of other's lives. Once we have done this, it will become easier to externalize those sentiments into manifestations of a clear, bright, & graceful conscience...

10:09 am 9/13

[KNIGHTS MOVEMENT] . . .

THEN ::

I Am the Law

I AM the Law. I got it medicine. Declaiming the superficial wisdom; and they don't realize the likeness that's blinded all of the New.
     We had the game to understand the game...
No Lands came before me.
No Bros & Chicks to be sticking it . . . a smokescreen around our media outlets
Watch me explode with impersonal disgust
  Impersonal catalepsy, never personal, how do I learn how not to trust?
How to I learn to hate?
The law wins; precedent over popular opinion, nothing in God to gauge.
Nor, too, the will of the motto. Fuck the public opinion trajectory, Brothers,
  there ain't no winning at work, or really this ~ any kind of lotto.
And the Law say: "Time Stops for NO MAN".
Fucka!!

Smoking Hookah & dUh Old Timer's Show

Old Man: I have ONE line for YOU, Kid.
Me: Wha's that?

"Sometimes a man's gotta do, what a man's gotta do - EVEN IF he doesn't know WHY."

Metaphysics Sloppy Book I Page # 364 - Derailed

 (Synesthesia - AUTOMATIC Poem)

O ArgooooOoOooo Argooo? . . , - (bleh ---- 98 7 34 32 2p kdnkdfmlsj 12jpf
OoOOooOooɔOo
Laze, Goooong, stylist she sho lit frame soft gentle touch motif tame tuned
wooooooooooooosh
~aromatic~ adrift
Soos sallowsss sallowwww seee sallowwww sallowww Seeeeeesss.....
uncowelled ranks, void as tanks,
airplane victory ride celebration same same different, true and truth
Argo, Argo, Argo Argo puncture gun shot blew
exquisite assemeble ensemble dutiful yell
the loudness of elegant knell

Gonnnnnnnrnnnnnnnnng!

The Roman Bath a.k.a. Bathtub for Unclean Infantes (Numba 2)

The only dirty water I will submit to be drowned or bathed in
 is the mythic sea of incontrovertible fortune
For it is the only dirty water that cleanses beyond
 comprehension and leaves no trace of filth, ah, but all bathtubs are left with filth.

BAPTIZE ME, O, Shepards!! And Franciscan Monks!
  Wont for long?

  . . . I don't want to be buried.
I want birds to eat me corpse while I lie rotting in a fucking field.

[Perfect & Grotesque]

But what else could be realistically said?
The funeral of life is the death of the soul and the failure to fly

...& the preference is a breathing tapestry with more harmony & grace
  than the totality of the High Renaissance ~

Time Destroys Us All.

Wisdom is wasted on the young; and Youth is wasted on the Wise

/////////////////////////

Time DestroyS US ALl

TIme Destroys us All
TIME DESTROYS US ALL!!

TIME Destroys Us aLL

time destroys us all!!
time destroys us all.

S & I Again Speak to Sara

Whence the tomb pries lashes shut
& soggy eyes do cease, there beams a corner
light entombed, which deprives & upsets
as the Death Rots yr Auburn hair
& a whirl of icy chill enchants & haunts
thru the midnight hour, sentience embodied & lifeless still
passed thru an omnipresent nothingness . . .

And then, in my darkest nights despair
I sing the most songs to everything
 For I miss Sara and her perfumed hair
 Now we'll go accept eternity's anything

Forget prior confusion and failings
I know that death does human rot
Minus our sickness, and ailing
mere body and its mortal plot

Moving on the breadth of time
To fly on the wings of the night!

e.e. cummings poem

comma. word. second word. semi-colon.
    non-sensical lyrics. upside down concrete verbiage.
  space space space ....;; ooiiejfjf 03923 a. ?!
vertical hierarchy of poetry - shit flows down hill
    . . . and no sense follows.
everything in lower case

Pizza Shop BrO

My Brother managed a Pizza Shop fohr YEARS.
He used to play games like get Mark drunk.
    He used to have competitions with employees about who could box boxes faster.
    He rocked dat shit. a FUCKING PRO.
Listening to Alice and Chains Unplugged. HELL YES!
There's a certitude to all this craziness, a beautiful serenity and walking away
    at the end of the day, knowing you leave it behind you until tomorrow.
Ain't like white collar work - where you never leave the office and stroke out at 40.
Should ye unionize? Well, really, unions cut BOTH ways, truth be told.
    Depends on the work &
ONE'S EMPLOYER!!
    But shit man, necklace dangling from my neck, all tattooed up...
    I Burned My Fucking Hand on the Pizza Rack today. That shit's gonna welt up.

But hey, pizza is still pizza, my fucking brilliant, magnificent bro!!

Others, English, and the Anti-Philology of Foucault (I, & II)

Part I.

    How the FUCK did Michel Foucault write all of his stuff?! I mean, there's like
1,000 pages and then there like THREE sources! Like, what the FUCK?! How the FUCK
did this happen?!

Part II.

PROBLEMS WITH THE INEFFICIENCY OF THE ENGLISH LANGUAGE (FROM A
LINGUIST'S VIEW) ::

Oh, I'm a Ph.D. educated English professor. Call me DOCTOR, dammit!
    Oh, you misused a comma!? Oh FUCK! No you didn't! That's it! Minus ten
points!
You're going to die poor and LONELY!! WHAT THE FUCK?!! Ending a sentence in a
preposition?

Your life is over. You're done. Just give up. You'll never get laid.
everything is finished for you. No job. No money. Just death. You used a preposition and no footnotes.
It's amazing. You truly astonish me. Like you SUCK! I don't think you're even worthy of life because of that.

Wait!! Did you JUST WRITE A SENTENCE FRAGMENT?!!

Motherfucker, you may as well just go kill yourself.

And why, teach. would I exactly want to study something as inefficient, arbitrary, and banal as the English language?

I SAID I HAVE A Ph.D.

.....Yes, m'am. I'm going to go buy a revolver and blow my brains out.

DOES ANYONE ELSE WANT TO WRITE A SENTENCE FRAGMENT? Hmmm?!!!

About this mysterious woman!

About this mysterious woman's storm!
 If thee I must forever follow
Your hours faltering & needing more
 Or bringeth wet rains temperate woes!

I cannot compete in thine girly wake
 And I know woman doth always face
Wounded ears & a dissuaded fate breaks
 Upon that crooked purse & plain lace

To A Buoy

Water'd and canst on thy float'n raft
Yelled abyss'n great swells
Lobsters shouts the fallen windy draft
Dress'n a vessel's hold

Mid-Sea—fights snugly graviton
Depths congeal n' hide Leviathan
And peaceful you were on
top o' crafty wafts n' Seas

like a marker of Roman Miles

guard the floatin' Seas
there, upon the Seaweed, grins
We've lost not a whim!

/////////////////////////////

Journal Entry # ?

     I feel like Dickie - ya know? Micky Ward's brother from Lowell, Massachusetts?
I don't know why.
And that's neither an insult.

     It's a strange compliment . . .
I am no longer lost in New England. I am found someplace else. Fuck.

/////////////////////////////////

People who can go through life without becoming shell-shocked make me jealous.

//

People can be so mean sometimes. I like to think that all human beings are
fundamentally decent.
     But lately, I'm thinking Bertrand Russell was right -- except not about man's
rationality;
  but rather, the opacity in Orwellian double-think of women . . .

facepalm

////////////////////////////////

YOUNG TIMER: I'm going to high school so I can go and get my diploma
          so I can go off and join the Marines!

(Old Timer pays for his meal at the Deli)

OLD TIMER: Do you know how to win a war, boy?

YOUNG TIMER: No. How?

OLD TIMER: You don't go to war to begin with.

MoRt the Poeta, Appellation Sex Exhaust

As the poet shed his medallions
His raw annoyance seeks to release
A peach'd tongue & diffident, blue eyes
As his frenchified soulgirl moans---
Near on a trance, kisses her sores & thighs
Thru blemishes o'er a circular toil
Candles beginning to crumble & cry
& in Her slow caress he feels an
Endless exert of a desire to sigh

Critical Discourse Pyramids

This is the language-oriented breaking laws.
 Never slaves to the philosophy
Corrupted motherfuckers . . . this means "language' rules
And language follows rules, by default.
A revolution amidst the brushfires in Colorado
        Call me Mr. Linguist
and fuck the appellation "Ph.D."
  Population is sick, we're starting a linguistic-critical discourse studies WAR
Sixteen grad students, pens, and typewriters
Fuck limited command of language.
        It's all a spiritual and religious calling.
A sacramental vocation.
 Yea.
Stimuli abroad and the inverse, like the memory chip implanted in Kip's Brain.
We know the feeling.
Rabies shit . . . but not that Zeus-like dictatorship.
    Oft times ostracize post-apocalyptic molecular regimes
Gods who often do this . . . their immediate nature is in dispensational
dead in dormant psychosis N.O.S. - helicopters only last for so long
So too...do the idealogues and spaceships on the News.

Ready?

Gimme the fucking typewriter, meng.

Aspects of the Futility of Syntax

...Everyone should just give up studying syntax. Chomsky already did that shit. Syntax is done. It's over. He took it to its limits. You can't do shit with it. It's done. THAT'S ALL!!

Smashing Pumpkins

Dude, Smashing Pumpkins ROCK.
    (exhales L) : No SHIT.

///////////r/////////////

Could you imagine a debate between Donald Trump and Hillary Clinton?

Just listen to Bobby D. - You're a punk, a bozo, a moron, and an embarrassment.

    Aughn...
Just watch SNL. Alec Baldwin is SPOT ON;

And then the election simply becomes haunted by the Specter of Trump! Yet who really would "win"?
    *I am afraid of calling myself an American...while ineffectually-privileged, wannabe authoritarian kleptocratic buffoons are frontrunners! *cry* :(*

O, Archangels, sing!! Sing and Pray for America! O, Americana! Americana!

~ If you were to scrape the bottom of a bowl in a bong free from narcissism, gunk, bully, dumbassness jackassery, racism, sexism, and xenophobia (among lots of other "undesirable" things) . . . DONALD TRUMP WOULD (invariably) BE THE RESIN!!
    . . . And then I'd flush that shit down the toilet; where it BELONGS!

////////////i/////////////

Alexej: We should get some real Kansas City BBQ!

Stephen: Hell yeah man. Point the way.

///////////i/////////

I FUCKING HATE "ENGLISH" MAJORS!!

/........................../

VATICAN

```
----------------------------------------------------------------------> = <---------------->
```

A Crying Virgil

Sharpened apt. stretch'd mirror is cracked
I haven't lived an affair in years
My image is a lice referred
Laughing an awful lot about rural jewels
Taking Troy is an endeavor of fire
My bearings need regrouping & oiling
Flying on brooms to sweep empty clouds
& all things gather dust
Music's nomenclature purifies ancient tools
Steeped in libraries full of glyphs
Harmonics gasp in dumb eras of Italy
The Pope breathes an unstained grave
Gathering the homeless playing harps
A fancy fantasy dumb utopian Raphael
Hath you sleep in your birthday cake?
Our guide is woe & envisioned
He demonstrates a faculty for high art
And illustrates God's reflection in his image

Noam Chomsky Word Salad

The foundational apparatus of institutionalized control was certainly in the broader schematic of
        say the underlying structure or model of U.G. or generative grammar. In the broader hypothesis
of say, the sundering of minority-autonomy, there is overwhelming historical precedent in say, the 100 years war if we examine the statistical data analysis the fundamental elements, properties, or aspects of U.G. or generative grammar we find the post-zionist literature through the lens of critical discourse studies and Descarte's unfinished work on the mathematical model of the human mind through dispensational analyses. Now, man had no intuitive, internal understanding of say the gravitational constant, however, he did understand the rational, computational basis for the C-1 interface with say, the science of the psychology of linguistic-detailed study. Further, the sensory-stimuli system is a finite system and should be addressed accordingly. The organizational language hierarchy was indexed by the cumulative hierarchical model in set theory per Von Neumann certainly in the 19th century. The transformational grammar was adequate for supplying the syntactic structures of U.G. and proved to be of infinite use

for the minimalist programs. According to something like X-Bar theory, where A.M. Turing believed A.I. to replace the clocks of Galileo the syntax-semantic interface is deemed germane certainly by the rationalist standards of post-Leninist doctrine.

However much Piaget may have shied away from various empiricist tendencies we do find a certain amount of latitude in the Israeli-Palestinian conflict; which is precisely what U.S. intelligence analyzes -- now, this is a direct attack on Obama. Congress is sending a message to the breakdown of society through a means by which no direct correlation can be made to any anthropological hegemony; certainly as it relates to the sundering of overall autonomy in the broader schematism of creativity or linguistic novelty. Matsou and I discussed these topicalities in an interview in Paris in the 1970s. The New Mandarins proved inadequate in scope and time to stave off the immutable travesty of the creativity of justice versus power and the inevitable and bizarre debate with Michel Foucault. The electronic reality of the modern era is certainly owed to the consent of the consumer placed by profit over people, which is a fundamental aspect or property of U.G. or generative grammar. And as for generative poetics, I cannot discuss -- as I had nothing to do with that social mapping in the instantiation of the claim's identity-formation, conversely the infinite, and now undefined parameters of generative semantics. As a corollary, the physicist examines nature, though mathematics are an underlying aspect of linguistic deployment and performance. The post-Cartesians could not be concerned with the mathematical-physics of Pascal, certainly not in the realm of what came after. Now, 500 years of scientific inquiry has proved utterly substantial. Which is a fundamental aspect of U.G. or generative grammar, and Occupy Wall Street has been a good thing for Democracy and we'll just have to see where it goes . . .

Neurotics

I'm not afraid of food poisoning; I'm afraid of Bovine Spongiform Encephelopethy
I'm not afraid of death; I'm afraid of gamma ray bursts
I'm not afraid of pregnancy; I'm afraid of penile cancer from a bizarre strain of HPV
I'm not afraid of computer viruses; I'm afraid of the electrical grid being wiped out
I'm not afraid of identity theft; I'm afraid of identity crises
I'm not afraid of finances; I'm afraid of global economic meltdowns
I'm not afraid of the flu; I'm afraid of airborne, incurable diseases
I'm not afraid of Death; I'm afraid of solar flares.

One might say there is a neuroses to being CAREFREE. Almost paranoid or paranoiac about one's egghead, batshit artistry and everything that follows with an otherwise ODD brain...I doubt phrenology would be useful here . . .

TBD . . .

The Homeless Sailor, XXS

My sailor friends have just left beguiled, reptile, ~ Hungary
I am left with some bricks of sexy hash and a sock full of kief
Now I have no home, not even a BOAT!
I wish I could once again peruse the Indian Ocean and take issue with that blasted, infernal Java
Like I did many times before! The Egyptian women meant nothing to me
Nor, too, did France's expensive wines!
But I have also broached the several pirates of a contradictory coordinate course
They take umbrage at my unorthodox discourse
I have set my head on the plushest of pillows
and felt the caress of sexy Egyptians
Smoked the finest marijuana, the finest tobacco
and injected the Persian dope with clean, clean, syringes
But everyday is an exercise in chaos!
I totally have spent countless hours, inestimable, unfathomable
. . . but I am not ashamed
My principles do not halt, fall or collapse like poorly constructed architecture
When God permits and Ra willing he will knight me, the knight of the Sea

The Hard Truth [And Make Your Peace With It]

Time stops for no Man.
And that's a hard sell;
        a timeless Hell.
Life is a room full of Death.
        And there is no God in here . . .

I am the Unincorporated Poeta. I eat my crappy food in the tenements bought
with food stamps. But I eat. And I read. And I create.
        Ideally, I come out strong like Langston Hughes.
Q.E.D.

Proverbial Variation # III

Life is like a river of time. And if we're not careful, we might drown.

/////////////

Fedallah

Fedallah's ruptured the Colossal Claw
He hast stricked vast & ignoble Beasts!
He stands erect in a turban & flowing Purple Robes
        a sash & Parscee Ascot, --- Harpoon in Right Hand!
Looking out to infinite Seas . . .
Zoraster exalts Ormazd!
But Ahriman is fortified in Steel
As Hearses approach by no mortal means
Reins of Black Hawks meet civil honors
Leviathan speaks its fetid noise
Asherah knows not of Yojo!
But Campagna & swamps is no match for the Sahara; cries God:

That which Consumeth Man, Consumeth All!

Proverbial Variation # IV

Stoner # 1 - Floyd is still, and will always be, better than Zeppelin.
    Stoner # 2 - No fucking way, man. Righteous. Hey, do you think that Zeppelin was called Zeppelin because Keith Moon was high when he said Lead Balloon?

Stoner # 1 - Yeah, man. And Keith Moon knew it would take off. That's why he took pills, man.

    Stoner # 2 - Oh shit. That's some fucking crazy shit, man.

The "right-wing" is too stupid. And the "left-wing" is too ideological.

////////////////////

Life is a neverending series of "should-have's".   :(

////////////////////

Idealism is the drug of youth. Cynicism is the toxin of old age.
    Idealism is the last refuge of the clueless. Cynicism is the last vestige of a deteriorating intellect.

////////////////////

BrothaBear called my ex-girlfriend a sociopath. I'm beginning to agree.

You know, the type of chick that could work any guy in the room, and who knew it?

It was really awesome! We were getting to know each other, there was this rapport;

everything was going so fast -- I felt this incredible affinity and affection.

There was all this sexual tension - it was amazing!

Then, after a manic meltdown - she realized she couldn't *escape* with me, so she treated me like an object and left.

Brothabear says: "Yeah. A sociopath."

And I'm just like: "Everyone says that!" BUT . . .

#SOCIOPATHS MAKE THE BEST LOVERS!!

They Were Mighty

"The Promise of America IS America"

The "They Were Mighty" screenplay was originally written about a group of mid-twenty somethings: Mikey, Syd, Stark, Duff, & P.J. - it was going to be PURE AMERICANA.

It was to be filmed in all black & white, with an opening quote from Langston Hughes with a dreamy, poetic motif - B & W baseball AMERICANA juxtaposed against Michael Balfe's Opera - "I Dreamt I Dwelt in Marble Halls".

Kind of like the Raging Bull thing; only even more poetic.

The soundtrack included (largely) Bruce Springsteen's 2012 "Wrecking Ball" album - amid the quiet revolutions and cultural epiphanies of 2012.

The music would have been anachronistic.

In was set in 1940's Michigan, where a group of delinquents (Mikey, Stark, Syd, Duff, and P.J.) would be five similarly minded and similarly ambitious working class kids in a thriving manufacturing and farming area 100 miles outside of Detroit.

They wouldn't be interested in finishing high school knowing they want to be laborers and workers though their parents and siblings have different ambitions. Though they have personality and ambitions that are similar they come from different backgrounds - Mikey is the one with a shot at college and a slightly sensitive, albeit, dissolute Christian, half-intellectual; Stark is a charming but volatile guy without much interest in productivity; Syd is contemplative but adventurous; Duff is the eccentric; and P.J. is a knockaround seemingly invincible guy - all from poor families diverse in size, and housing facilities, the sense of community is strong, only Stark and Syd have girlfriends and P.J. frequently strays.

Only a few of their families are close friends, but all are known to each other, while of a similar socioeconomic bracket, their stories are all very different. P.J. is more of a farmboy; Stark's entire family works in food service; his Father owning a bar, Syd's family in an automotive factory; Mikey's fairly upper class parents are temporarily unemployed; and Duff is from a foster home.

One thing they live and do religiously is gather at a decripet field to play baseball every chance they get, they are strong [ergo, - MIGHTY] and very talented but disorganized, rude, and abrupt. They are the youthful kings of their modest kingdom of working class midwest small towns in an emerging America.

They are the center of everything and mean everything to a group of people, a small group [mostly young kids who come to watch them play ball] but their impact on one another is tremendous.

As they aspire to play professional baseball they simultaneously try to raise money to go see a series of Tigers games in Detroit and court their girlfriends.

EVEN TO SEE JUNE 15th, 1948 AT TIGER STADIUM! [Detroit's first nightgame].

. . . and trying to impress their dates if they can get to the game, they meanwhile begin hosting spectacular feats of balltricks for the entertainment of younger high schoolers and their younger siblings, thus abandoning school altogether.

How their lives impact, and intersect across family, friends, love, and interests, and how their ambition affects the progress of once modest and earnest dreams in the face of their ignorant outsider life and the medical and emotional reverses would be at the heart of this ecumenical American masterpiece.

They would get to the game - at their worst and at their best . . .

The film would end with "American Land" by Bruce Springsteen, with an underlying motif of "RETIREMENT" . . . once the fellas realize they can't hack it as professional ballplayers and need to move on.

"For any a workingman . . . we made our Home in the American Land."

In the final scene, Syd would stare at their sandlot, as the song played, and then tip his Tigers hat, grin, with certitude and sentimentality, and then walk away forever.

Aerial Shot of the city as the credits roll to the music. SUBLIME.

FADE OUT :

//////////////////////////////////

Life is a sucker punch to the gut.

//////////////////////////////////

Gibberish

hish hash ee - O yeahm, duhk, lots, blaeh.

...........and there is no need to know the time; WE ARE TIMELESS!!!

/////////////////////////////////

THE GREATEST LESSON IS THAT SOMETHING CAN ALWAYS BE LEARNED!!

... you say you love

YOU SAY YOU LOVE YET MANY SHIPS HAVE YET TO SAIL, & BACTERIA IS STUCK IN THE DRAIN OF TIME

YOU SAY YOU LOVE LIKE A YOUNG COUPLE BUT THE COMEDY RIDES LIKE AN ILLOGICAL CLIME

YOU SAY YOU LOVE TO LICK THE TONGUES OF A DYSPHORIC HUNGER YET PANGS STILL A-BREATHE

YOU SAY YOU LOVE TO BE FREE YET YOU NEVER CHASE AFTER THE UNFATHOMABLE, ECUMENICAL SEA

YOU SAY YOU LOVE YET YOU KISS THE CHASTE, A LOVE SO TRUE TO BE CONDEMNED UNFREE

YOU SAY YOU LOVE LIKE A DEVOUT & SCANDALOUS NYMPH & THE
MASQUERADERS MOCK YOU!

YOU SAY YOU LOVE YET YOU HAVE YET TO WRITE MYSTERY &
HOLISTIC & ABERRANT ANTHEM

YOU SAY YOU LOVE LIKE THE PATRIOTS & DADDIES OF THE AGE YET
VITRIOL CONQUERS & YE SHAKES

YOU SAY YOU LOVE YET THOSE SHIPS YOU COMMANDEER, ARE
ALWAYS SLY AT PORT & QUAY

YOU SAY YOU LOVE LIKE THE ARCHANGELS IN DEFEAT, YET NO HEART
BEATS & MELTS LIKE EPHEMERAL WAX

YOU SAY YOU LOVE BUT ONLY TIL THE LANTERN IS THROWN AGAINST
SOME STONES & CATCHES HELL

YOU SAY YOU LOVE BUT YOUR CAR WON'T EVER CATCH STUCK IN THE
MUD LIKE A FATTISH ADDICT

YOU SAY YOU LOVE THE SUICIDAL CLOWN & THE BROKEN COOK, BUT SMOKE IN THE GUTTER LIKE A ROACH

YOU SAY YOU LOVE ALL THRU THE RAW BLIGHT PAST, THE PALELY LIT CORRIDOR OF AN EMOTIONAL FAST

YOU SAY YOU LOVE IN THE MIST OF SAD HORMONAL BREATHS & UNTIL YOU KILL & THE UNDIGNIFIED CROAKS

YOU SAY YOU LOVE ALL IN A BREATH, CHOKING ON YOUR ADIOS BLOOD & TURNING ASHTRAYS INTO CASKS

I'll Never Feel as Good as I did when I was 23

I'll never feel as good as I did for four magical months when I was 23.
      God, I doubt even you could pull another rabbit out of the hat.

</3.

/////////////////

     PEOPLE WHO ARE TRUE ORIGINALS ARE OFTEN MISUNDERSTOOD :/

///////////////////////////////////

For Emil; who Survived Mauthausen, & His Daughter's Family

Us humans, condemned forever to sail
In the throes of a foul-weather gale,
  Through cloudy billows like a harpoon
As love bends o'er time's stage
& soon traces the damned & the saved
& thy love is bartered with hallelujahs

Sweet scene of thy blatant illuming truths!
Seat of old age & ephemeral youth,
Where time chases thy fleeting tune
  Loth to leave thee, & mirthfully mourn
For a last look we shall but once return
  As thy spirit fulfills e'ermore with a hallelujah

Though said vows are fragile, they sow
  All my farewells I said so long ago
My loneliness increas'd & appear'd so soon
But I remember truthfully choosing
As the lone fragrant, shadow was diffusing
  God rewarded ye with mighty hallelujahs

By another soul's inquisitive behest
She doth e'er feel so softly blessed
  Her time I knew withdrew in awe
With a state of pride I doth decide
What I thought I saw in time resides
  & entrusted ye with a hallelujah

When my soul uses thy wings to flight
To thy ethereal regions of haughty height
  & my course shall determine my union;
As ye go to & fro about thy swoon
Whence all my thoughts doth consume,
  O! Askance their truce lying in a hallelujah

May no horrid pensive frown o'ertake
Thy grandeur I see adamantly endear
  Which your fruitful grandchildren knew you;
No chance restriction doth e'er deceive
For love blazeth thy past & yet once more believe
  I alone control all my undying hallelujahs

///

Winston Churchill (or somebody like him) was reputed to have said something like:
"If you're not a liberal at twenty, you have no heart. And if you're not a
conservative by forty, you have no head."

Well, I reject this. In a world that can be so unabashedly and morally bankrupt,
the only real currency worth treasuring is the content of the human heart.

///////////////

THE BOOK'S NEW CHAPTER::

. . . . .

Ya know man . . . I don't know that you say "goodbye" *twice*.

[CM] : . . . I could see that.

///

My FINAL conversation with a nice female therapist:
She calls out to me as she opens her door and I walk down a side hallway:

"Don't be afraid to be interesting. Don't be afraid to be *yourself*."

Epilogue

Is it really so noble to die believing in nothing?

www.ingramcontent.com/pod-product-compliance
Lightning Source LLC
Chambersburg PA
CBHW030540290526
45786CB00004B/1786